HI THERE!
Welcome.
Hey, listen, if you don't give a shit about dedications or
introductions; if you're one of those, "instructions are
suggestions" or "just show me the goods already" types,
you may want to skip right to page 6. It is a kind, sweet
intro though; if I do say so myself.
Either way.
You're welcome. Love you, too.
Enjoy!

Love, Ami

Welcome to the life of a child who likes to write. Some might say that self-expression is the key to success, with which I would agree, but this book is not just a collection of self-expression. This book is a journal, a collection of thoughts, feelings, emotions, and experiences; a journey through every part of me that I dare not speak of. You, now, may embrace this through paper and pen. I can only hope that some of these words reflect some of your own and that somewhere here you find a small shred of hope and happiness; know that you're not alone; and feel as I do, that we are sharing this together. Everyone's journey is their own and for mine, I want you with me.

I ask you now to open your mind and your heart; take a walk with me; hold my hand.

Dedication

For My Mommy. I miss you, Always.

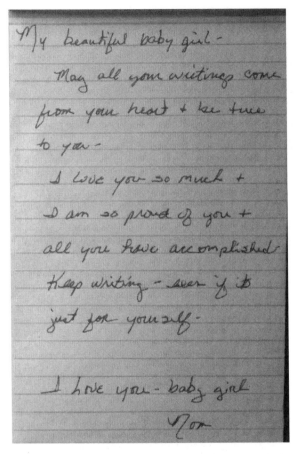

My beautiful baby girl -

May all your writings come

from your heart + be true

to you -

I love you so much +

I am so proud of you +

all you have accomplished

Keep writing - even if it's

just for yourself -

I love you - baby girl

Mom

Mom, you taught me everything I could ever need to know and most importantly, that it was in me all along. You were my best teacher, toughest coach, and kindest guide. Words will never be enough. I love you so much and yes, I know you love me more. Thank you for helping me become empowered enough to truly and deeply speak, write, and share from my heart space. I would not exist this way without your love and spirit living in me the way you do.

3

Just so you know:

The highlighting you will see here is from my Mommy.

My Mother told me for years and years to publish my poems, to share them, and I always said no.

Well. Then she got diagnosed with stage 4 stomach cancer. And when that happens you really, really will do anything. She asked again for me to publish my poems and so I did – quickly! Luckily, I was able to get a draft printed before she passed away, so she was able to read it.

After she passed, I found her copy in her things with these lovely little notes and highlights and comments.

I assume those are the parts she really liked, and I can hear her in my head going, "Yes!" and "That's right," as I read with her highlights. I hope you hear her too. She is the only reason I put 25 Years of Words together in the first place.

I wanted to share those notes with you. You will see them.

I also dedicate this book to all those that took me in and loved me when I thought I was alone and those that were there all along, even when I couldn't see. To anyone who has ever cared for me, loved me, accepted me, supported me, and those that hate me, or hurt me; each a guiding light and inspiration in your own right. To all those very special hands that have touched my life and helped to mold my heart. To my moms, dads, brothers, sisters, lovers, and friends; you are truly irreplaceable. I love you all eternally. Thank you.

A few F.Y.I.s for you

(This is like the "please watch your flight attendant show you how to use a seat belt" moments. You don't need to watch but you always do anyway...ya know, just in case they've invented some new state of the art seat belt that only 10-year olds know how to work – oh wait, that's cell phones, my bad.)

So, when you see "S.N." it signifies a "Side note": an additional comment added in this version and not an original part of the poem/work, but fun anyway. To be even MORE fun, please enjoy added "Fun Facts" as well. Those are self-explanatory, yeah? Hope so.

You didn't know this version was going to come with a "how to read this book" section, did you? Sorry, not sorry. And again, you're welcome. Is it obvious I'm a little nervous and stalling a little bit? No? Good, because that would be silly, right? Right. Okay, good then. Fine.

Oh, P.S. in the words of a dear, dear friend:

"I love Jesus, but I curse a little." -Tess Ponce

And by a little, I mean a lot. I am, indeed, classy as fuck. You've been warned.

Let's do this!

Here we go...deep breath.

GO!

LET THE POETRY.....BEGIN!

High school speech assignment.

I am particularly proud of this one, Enjoy.

Declaration of Independence

2005

When in the course of human events it becomes necessary for one people to dissolve the standards and expectations that society has set of what a person of a specific gender should be, a decent respect to the opinions of mankind requires that they should declare the causes, which impel them to the separation. I hold these truths to be self-evident, that those of the female gender are not necessarily long-haired, skirt and make-up wearing people, that they are all endowed by this great nation to dress, speak, and conduct themselves in any manner they so choose. Though society has drawn conclusions and expectations due to magazines and models or exactly what a girl should be, that is not the case. Nor is that the case for those of the male gender either.

"For every girl that throws out her Easy Bake Oven, there is a boy wishing to find one. For every girl who is tired of acting weak when she is strong, there is a boy tired of appearing strong when he feels vulnerable. For every boy for whom competition is the only way to prove his masculinity, there is a girl who is called unfeminine when she competes. For every boy struggling not to let advertising dictate his desires, there is a girl facing the ad industry's attack on her self-esteem."

The history of society's attacks proves the repeated injuries of self-esteem and confidence towards people today. To prove this further, let facts be submitted to a candid world.

Pointing his finger, He tells girls and women that if they are not slim they are not worthy of love.

He tells boys and men if they are not buff and muscled they are not worthy.

He makes empty promises over and over again of a better life through some new product or surgery to make you a better man or woman.

He tells everyone that to be a woman you must wear short skirts and tight shirts.

He tells everyone to be a man you must work out and wear loose clothing.

He says girls must wear make-up to be beautiful.

He says men who wear make-up are wrong and odd.

He refuses to accept any persons that may not fit into his category of what a person should be, and he has passed this on to the rest of the country and world.

At no time has it ever been publicized or spoken by He, that a girl who chooses to wear baggy pants could still be an attractive female.

At no time has it ever been said by He, that men who cry or like dolls could still find their soulmate within a woman.

At no time has it ever been stated by He, that to be comfortable and natural is to be beautiful.

I ask you this: why must we conform to these ignorant expectations?

Why must we be who society claims we should be instead of who we really are?

He has made it virtually impossible to be in this nation and not be hit with such expectations and standards. It is very rare that someone speak out against these abominations against mankind. His oppression of self-expression and acceptance goes far beyond the lines drawn here, but I, as a citizen of this great country and as one of the female gender, will wear baggy clothes and have short hair.

I will speak out against society's standards and I will be beautiful while doing so. I, here, declare my independence from society's standards and expectations, as I pledge my honor to the belief that society does not form who a person should be, the people form what society should be.

SIDE-NOTE: Any gender for that matter, we know now there are many! Call me if you need an explanation/training about that.

FOR EVERY GIRL WHO IS TIRED OF ACTING WEAK WHEN SHE IS STRONG, THERE IS A BOY TIRED OF APPEARING STRONG WHEN HE FEELS VULNERABLE. FOR EVERY BOY WHO IS BURDENED WITH THE CONSTANT EXPECTATION OF KNOWING EVERYTHING, THERE IS A GIRL TIRED OF PEOPLE NOT TRUSTING HER INTELLIGENCE. FOR EVERY GIRL WHO IS TIRED OF BEING CALLED OVER-SENSITIVE, THERE IS A BOY WHO FEARS TO BE GENTLE, TO WEEP. FOR EVERY BOY FOR WHOM COMPETITION IS THE ONLY WAY TO PROVE HIS MASCULINITY, THERE IS A GIRL WHO IS CALLED UNFEMININE WHEN SHE COMPETES. FOR EVERY GIRL WHO THROWS OUT HER E-Z-BAKE OVEN, THERE IS A BOY WHO WISHES TO FIND ONE. FOR EVERY BOY STRUGGLING NOT TO LET ADVERTISING DICTATE HIS DESIRES, THERE IS A GIRL FACING THE AD INDUSTRY'S ATTACKS ON HER SELF-ESTEEM. FOR EVERY GIRL WHO TAKES A STEP TOWARD HER LIBERATION, THERE IS A BOY WHO FINDS THE WAY TO FREEDOM A LITTLE EASIER.

CrimethInc. Adapted from a poem by Nancy R. Smith. CrimethInc. Gender Subversion Kit #69-R. Copies of this poster are available individually and in bulk quantities from CrimethInc. Gender Assignment / PO Box 12998 / Salem OR 97309 or if wanting ain't your thing, go to www.crimethinc.com

Story of My Life

2004

I feel the tears behind my eyes,

As I sit and talk about my life;

All of the pain and suffering I feel.

Most people think it's so unreal.

They can't believe that someone like me,

Being the person, I've grown to be,

Has had so much tragedy, gone through so much;

Had a life so damn tough.

Never truly feeling loved,

By the ones that mattered most.

Constantly haunted,

By an ever-somber ghost.

Yelling and screaming every day,

"Oh well, that's life" is what I always say.

But sitting now telling, of my days and nights,

Makes me see that that's not right.

A child should not have to live in fear of coming home.

It isn't alright to feel completely alone;

To have to hide in a shell and take it all in,

Leaves me to wonder, where will it end?

Where will this lead? Where will I be?

What will all this hatred do to me?

I've come too far to give up now.

I guess I'll have to stick it out.

I can't let them hurt me or tear me down.

I have to show who I am, what I've found.

All the things I have been though and seen,

I have to use them to better me.

Her

2004

You all know her. The girl with your heart.

The first one you loved. The first one to tear you apart.

She's always so wonderful, And oh, so great at first.

Then you give her your all, suddenly it all gets worse.

You try to work through it. You love her too much to let go.

You know she still loves you. You can feel it in your soul.

By the way she looks at you, as you hold her close.

The good times are so good, but too soon they become ghosts.

Just like shadows of the past, she walks away with every part of you.

Your first love and your first hate. You'll always love her, you know it's true.

You all know her. The girl with your heart.

The first one you loved, the first one to tear you apart.

Forever My Heart

2004

Like the stars shine forever,

Forever will I,

Give you my heart,

For forever,

All time.

Side-note:

Yeah, yeah, I know stars die...collectively though; they
have and will always exist, right?!

I Walk Alone

2003

Scattered beings on every side, simply watch as I pass them by. With nowhere to go but a broken home. I drive on forever, forever unknown.

Like the vastness of the desert sky, the ocean runs in and out with the tide. The nothingness flow to and fro, like my soul: with no place to go.

A line of lights like the rim of my soul, searching and searching with no place to go. A light I wish I could be shown. For forever in darkness, I walk alone.

Photo Credit: Anne-Michelle

Like the Stars

2003

With the morning comes a new day so like the stars, I sink. Sink into the nothingness of the day to come.

Sink into the nothingness of what I have become.

Such a feeling of worthlessness consumes my heart and soul.

I can't control these feelings inside, I don't know why I am here.

Too soon do these feelings I abide and see my life as so unclear.

With the night comes another chance, so again I try to shine.

Try to find a meaning for mean, a reason to be without doubt. With the day, I sink, the night I rise to be: bright like that stars, until the day I burn out.

FUN FACT:
Around this time, I was REALLY into A.F.I.
(the band, Google it. Great stuff! To this day
Davey Havok - lead singer is my one dude I
wouldn't mind.) If you are familiar or listen to
a few songs, you'll get it. If you are Davey and
reading this, call me ☺

Tragedy is Tragedy

2003

With life in my hands and death in my grip, it all seems so worthless. Like one bad trip.

Tragedy is tragedy, there's no need to change. Just bathe in your sorrow, learn from the pain.

What is your life? Where will it lead?

If you died tonight, are you sure you would bleed?

Will you leave a stain or mark in this place?

Or will you walk away, the universe's disgrace?

Fight On

2004

A crash and a slash. I thought I died for sure. I felt a ton of blood, gushing to the floor.

Just then I stood up.

And slowly walked away.

All the blood wasn't mine.

I will live yet another day.

Through all the pain and sorrow, I feel. I know that one day, the scars will heal.

I will take what I am given.

Accepting the good and bad alike.

From now on I will be driven.

I will fight on for this life.

My most literal poem, I think.

FUN FACT:

My first car accident: I called my mom crying to tell her I hit someone. Her first thought was that I ran someone over – the F, Mom?!. I was trying to light a cigarette I was not supposed to be smoking, leaving a place I wasn't supposed to be, with a person I wasn't supposed to have in my car. I didn't tell Mom..or the cop any of that. My girlfriend at the time walked home before the police got there so I wouldn't lose my license or permit or whatever it was. Sorry girl! You the real MVP though.

Yeah, I know, right?

Broken Video

2004

I wish it would rain today.

Wash away all of my pain.

Take away this fear I hold inside, whisk me away into the night.

Playing over and over again in my head. Like a broken video, sometimes I'd rather be dead. But you have to hold on, hold fast to this life you see. There's always something out there, a reason to be happy and free.

When you're surrounded by so much hurt and pain, all you need is one slice of happiness just to make you see:

Life isn't as worthless as it used to be.

FUN FACT: Same girl from 2 pages ago, all "my first love" and shit (we dated for 4 months in high school, come on!) I was devastated at the time though. We are friends now – shout out!

Well, she went and broke up with me. I wrote this on tiny pieces of paper I found in my car, on the trunk of my car, while staring at the dark but bright sky. My response:

Falling Star

2004

I watched the sky tonight and saw a falling star. It reminded me so much, of my broken heart.

I thought of you and I don't know why. I thought of us and I started to cry.

I felt like the life, was drained from my soul. Without you, I fear, I'll never be whole.

It's been so long, but it feels like merely a day. Since we said goodbye, and my dreams washed away.

The love of my life, gone just like that.

For a little while after, I thought you had come back.

But you took my heart and won't let it go. So, I'll continue to live, the rest of my days in sorrow.

I tried so hard to be, good to you and true. But you ran away, why? Because you loved me too.

You loved me too and you didn't know why. I could feel it in your touch, see it in your eyes.

While we laid together, there alone in the dark. You could feel love between us, through interlocked arms.

We were both so happy, like we'd never known. You thought it was just too good to be true, you had to make it end.

Before you got hurt and your heart scarred for life. I had no idea, thought you could be my wife.

I was so blinded by childish love, so much I could not see. All the little tricks and lies you told me.

I have to admit, it was a smart plan. Anyway, we both know, you're better off with a man...

You were scared to really love me because of what people said, it's alright now though, 'cause I have someone else in my bed.

Fun Fact: Remember that girl from two pages ago that I was super in love with and couldn't imagine living without? Well, yeah, this isn't about her.

And so, begins the "love chronicles" of my life (like Narnia, but not nearly as cool). Different players, but always the same game. You might notice some themes in the following, be mindful and let's see if you figure it out.

Without You

2005

I've shed tears for you, shared my fears with you. I can't sleep without you.

I've never cried for a girl, before you were in my life; but I cried for you, and I cried all night.

Dependent on drugs and alcohol I have become. When you're not beside me, my heart is numb.

I need to have you with me, even when we're at work.

Just knowing you'll come home to me, keeps away the hurt.

Knowing that I will have to lie down alone, makes the fall of tears begin. Promise me please, you'll never leave me again.

Because, I have shed tears for you, shared my fears with you. I swear, My Love, I can't even sleep without you.

Some Reflections on "Without You":

For the record, I acknowledge how unhealthy this is. You should too.

That's called co-dependency, not good Friends.

Also...probably not entirely true that I had never cried about a girl prior to this. Let's be honest....oh and also, also...I have always been a REALLY great sleeper, so that last part, also probably not true. I really love sleep so much. Sorry, not sorry.

My Muse

2005

You are my muse, muse of inspiration.

Yet you give me, so much devastation.

Devastating beauty, devastating grace.

The way you smell, the way we embrace.

Everything you do, every word you say.

Give me reason to live, yet another day.

When the moonlight hits your face and your eyes become
so bright.

That's when I know what my heart is saying is right.

Because you are my muse, whispering in my ear.

You give me such peace, whenever you are near.

What I must ask, just continue to inspire.

I promise you this, only you I will desire.

Context: Fun Fact: My first "actual" relationship was with a woman who has a middle name of Rose. That makes this cute right, like the tattoo on my arm. Yeah, right. LOL #liveandlearn (we're friends now and it was a good tattoo anyway so..oh well.) #notmadaboutit #shoutout!

A Rose for You

2005

Like a wilting rose, so does my heart.

Each time I'm with you, you take another part.

Don't think this isn't what I wanted, please.

I give you my everything and I give it willingly.

Like the fall takes the leaves from trees, you take my heart and soul; I give you all of me.

You are like the stem to my flower of love, never weathered.

All thoughts of pain and sadness disappear when we're together.

Even when we're apart, you have nothing to fear.

For forever I will love you, I will always be here.

I will be here, waiting for you to come home.

Never should you feel as if you're alone.

I am with you in your thoughts. I'm in your dreams and heart.

No matter time or distance, nothing can keep us apart.

Now every time you see a rose, I want you to think of me.

Freeze it in your mind because that's where I want to be.

Frozen in your heart and frozen in your mind.

So, we'll always be as one, for forever, all time.

Forever you have me completely, like an everlasting bouquet.

I promise to love and care and to miss you every day.

I miss you when I can't kiss you or see your beauty staring back at me.

But missing you is a good thing. That is the way it should be.

If absence makes the heart grow fonder, I don't know what I will do.

I'm truly not sure I could handle being away from you.

I suppose what it is, that I am trying to say is even when we're apart, it will be okay.

When you lay down to sleep just think of this:

How great it will be, when again we share a kiss.

Always remember,

Like a wilting rose, so does my heart.

Never could anything truly keep us apart.

Some Reflections on "A Rose for You":

The translation of "forever" to reality was about 3.5 years, but at 17 I think that seems about right.

Again, cute idea, though right?!? Great line in any case. #sucharomantic

There's that co-dependency again, not cool man, not cool....

30-year-old me to 17-year-old me: "PULL YOURSELF TOGETHER MAN!..

On second thought, you're fucking 17 – do you Boo."

Burning

2005

Why is it when I burn, I can't feel a thing? But when it comes to you, I swear I feel everything.

There's no way to escape or try to run and hide. No matter where I go, you're always on my mind.

I try to just ignore it and act like it's not true but anything I say or do, always comes back to you.

There's no way to control it or get it to calm down. When you're not with me, I wish you were around.

When I burn, I can't feel, and this is what I've found: it's because my heart is burning, burning 'cause it's bound.

I'm bound to you, My Love, by my hands and feet. My heart and soul are with you, every moment and every beat.

I've learned it can't be beaten and it will never go away. I have realized now, that I'll love you until my dying day.

You're stuck with me forever and I am stuck with you. We have no choices here, except to our hearts, be true.

I promise I'll stop running and I won't try to hide. If you stay here next to me, promise you'll be mine.

Promise me Love, you'll never leave me lonely. I will let my heart keep burning, burning for you only.

So Gone

2005

A feeling so different, one I can't describe.

I can't tell you how happy I am, to have you in my life.

At a time when I felt so alone and cold, I thought I'd die alone and old.

Then you came along like a beautiful ray of sunshine.

You brighten up my days, you light up my nights.

Sometimes it scares me so much, how amazing you are.

The love that I feel, I've never been gone so far.

I miss you when I'm not with you and that's odd for me.

I never want to let you go, that's not how I used to be.

Before you I thought love was a figment of the mind.

But all those thoughts are gone now that you're mine.

I could lay forever just staring at your smile.

The most wonderful time is when we're just together for a while.

I want you to know, this is all new for me too.

But I'll always be there, I truly do love you.

Letter to You

2005

Dear You,

    Hey, hello. How are you?

I hope you're doing great. This may sound a little strange, but I have some things to say.

I want you to know that no matter what you hear, I am a sweet person and I enjoy having you near.

Sometimes my reputation has a way of gathering lie. I'm not who people think I am. I don't just ruin lives.

If you take the time to talk to and get to know me, you'll see a different person. The loving person I can be.

Most say that I'm outgoing, but I am really very shy. That's why I can't just say this, a poem I must write.

I know that I don't know you, but I fall into your eyes.

I want to be there for you, give you my days and nights.

It's true that I am a flirt and I'll do that all my life, but you are the one I think about when I lay down at night.

I wish I wasn't like this, that I could just tell you how I feel. But when I start to care it scares me and that is real.

So please, all I am asking is for you to let me try.

I promise you this one thing, only happy tears you'll cry.

S.N: the last line could have been: "except to promise that's a lie." No one can "cure" anyone else of sadness. The F Ami. Don't make promises you can't keep, Bruh. Oh, to be young again 😊

Story

2005

Isn't it the story, the way it always goes?

A secret forbidden love, that of course, no one knows.

It all starts out so simple, all just innocent fun.

But once feelings start flowing, what is there can't be undone.

When lust suddenly turns into something more.

The object of that lust, you too soon do adore.

You start to want to see them, even though you know it isn't right.

You call to talk about nothing but talk about everything all night.

On the surface of your mind, you know that it is wrong, but in the depths of your heart you want to love them all night long.

You yearn to lay awake and watch them as they sleep.

Just the thought of such beauty, tends to make you weak.

But as Shakespeare wrote, oh so long ago:

No love like this can last, without a hint of sorrow.

A forbidden lust forms a bitter love. Where hurt is what the cards have dealt.

For every night when you separate, they go home to someone else.

You live a lie, this you know.

Yet you continue, to let your wild love grow.

No chance for salvation or another ending here.

It will have to be played out. Go through the hurt, the pain, the fear.

So, what's the ending to this story? No one knows, not even me.

For love is never easy, especially those which should not be.

All the rest will watch this story, as it does unfold.

You must live through it though, go, and do be bold.

S.N. Alright! I call bullshit. Listen little uh what, 17-year-old me. This whole thing is bullshit and anyone who claims to "looove" you...would not be going home to anyone else. Pull your head out of your backside (that means ass). Oh, and tell your "every relationship after this" self this shit, too. You need to know this.

P.S. Yes, we do know how it ends. You lose. Stop doing that. Do not be bold, I repeat, do not be bold! Thanks. K, love you!

My Thanks to You

2005

I know you will always be true,

so, my eternal love is my thanks to you.

I know through you I will continue to learn,

my thanks to you is to feel my love burn.

I know we have the zsa-zsa-zsu,

so, giving you butterflies forever is my thanks to you.

I know we'll spend forever together,

my thanks to you is to be there through whatever weather.

I know you'll never make me feel blue,

so, giving you my heart is my thanks to you.

I know you are always there for me,

my thanks to you is that I will also be.

I know you will always do what I need you to,

I will do the same as my thanks to you.

I know you will always make me smile and laugh,

my thanks to you is to make that last.

I know with my dreams, you wish me to pursue,

So, making yours come true is my thanks to you.

I know you'd never break my heart,

my thanks to you is to do my part.

I know we have closeness, nothing could undo,

so, my complete dedication is my thanks to you.

I know we will make it through it all,

my thanks to you is to catch you should you ever fall.

I know we never thought all of this would come true,

making things ever better is my thanks to you.

I know we will be judged and looked down upon,

my thanks to you is to keep us going strong.

I know I gave up some for you,

but you gave up a lot for me too,

so, proving our love is worth it is my thanks to you.

I know that this is true love,

my thanks to you is all of the above.

My Own Device

2005

There's been a murder here and I hold all the clues. I've spoken to the witnesses, heard all of their views.

I know the victim well and I know the weapon too.

But who do you prosecute when both killer and victim are you?

I am the victim of my own device, that is where I stand.

The fears that I hold inside, keep me from holding another's hand.

I'm not the victim, that is what most people see But, that's only because they know the murderous side of me.

WOW! Can we just acknowledge, that escalated quickly LOL

Went from "blah blah thanks, love you" to "I'm a terrible person" real quick.

Growing Up

2005

A beauty so young and yet so full of pain.

She is just learning that life is one big game.

Overcome with a feeling of being alone and lost.

No idea of what being found really costs.

Not sure of anything but thinks she knows it all.

Thinks the little things are what cause her to fall.

Never truly knowing that there's always more.

Never comprehending that hearts are always sore.

It doesn't get better or easier with time.

Her innocence is scarred, as once was mine.

I fear that day that she sees the truth.

For I know it will hurt her, it will hit her at her root.

I can only hope that she will find her way.

And that she knows I'm here, every single day.

Taylor

2005

Baby girl, I want you to know:

Whenever I'm feeling sad and alone, I stare at your picture for hours on end.

Suddenly, I feel happy again.

When you were born I felt it inside.

I even told your mom, "this one is mine."

She might be your mom, but I am sure your aunt.

No matter where you are, that is where I'm at.

You are never alone in this world, as long as I live.

And even when I'm gone, in your heart I will survive.

I love you, Taylor, more than you know.

And maybe one day, when you are all grown,

You'll understand what I say to you now.

What a savior you are, the love that I've found.

Just when I thought I was all out of love,

You came into the world like an angel from above.

My advice to you, precious little girl, is to never give up.

You can conquer this cruel world.

Follow your heart and always do what you know is right.

Know that it is you that has to sleep at night.

Also, never forget that I am here

No matter where you are, know that I am near.

I keep you in my heart and in my thoughts, it's true.

Taylor Lynn, such a lovely little girl. I love you.

Blake

2005

To me you are the best.
Undaunted, truly fearless.

Every time I'm around you,
There's a security and truth that I know.
Every inside jokes we have told,
Secrets of the other we hold.

My best friend in the world.
Obdurate at times, it's true.
No one could mean to me as much as you.

A friend forever is what you'll find in me.
My faith, my trust, my friendship...
I give you my loyalty.

A poem I write, just to share my thoughts.

Just another way for me to try to show.
Another day that our friendship grows.
Millions of people go through their lives,
And never find a friend like mine.

I want you to know that here, there's something to find...
See the first letter of every line.

(Tu Etes Mon Ami A Jamais – You are my friend forever)

Why, (For Dad Part 2)
2006 (18 years old)

Why is it that I yearn for you, but you've forgotten about me?

Why do I miss you so, but you've chose for this separation to be?

Why do I cry constantly for you, but you don't shed any tears?

Why are we so distant, but you deny your fears?

Why am I so proud of you, but you still deny me as your child?

Why are you so scared, but won't just fight these trials?

Why do I hold so strongly, but you seem to have just let go?

Why do you claim to love me but refuse to let it show?

Side-note: It hurt me a lot to type this in recent times because my Dad has been so good to me. I am happy to report that even though it took a while and some mis-steps on both of our parts, Dad and I get along so well, and we are super close, like when I was young. We are more alike than not and have great adventures together. We grow together.

Never Say Die

2006

Every day I wake up, I suffocate. Every time I close my eyes, my heart just fills with hate. My existence is sacred, no one seems to know. But every day inside me, my hatred grows and grows. What kind of life is this, for a child to have to live? So much hurt, fear, and pain. So many people left to forgive. Too much tension building up in my heart. Stress is extreme but it's impossible to break apart. I can't just give up or fall apart like others can. For some reason, I am too strong. Failure is just not in the plan. So, I suppose I will continue, continue to wake up and suffocate. For I know I will survive, I will live out a better fate.

No 'One'

2009 – 21 years old (in case you weren't counting)

The one, the one, what is "the one"?

Who and why and where?

Why does she matter?

Why should I care?

What if she's a myth?

A legend in my mind.

What if "the one" doesn't exist?

How am I so blind?

I thought I had found my "one" once,

Or maybe it was twice.

To think you know what love is,

It's absurd in my mind.

To live with one person,

For fifty or more years?!

How can anyone make that?

Masking all the tears.

No one is perfect,

And surely neither am I.

So, finding the "one"

Simply must be a lie.

It must be a façade,

I can't believe it's not a lie

No one can be the one,

Not forever, not for all time.

Guilty

2009

Why do I feel nothing?

Why do I not sink?

Why do I not cry?

All I do is think.

I need pain in my life.

I need it like air.

I need to feel heartbreak.

To know that I still care.

Why can't I focus?

Why can't I see you in my mind?

Why can't I feel you linger?

All of these, combined.

I know that I loved you.

I know that you were true.

I know that we had something,

But I'm cold all the way through.

There's nothing there.

I don't know why.

I stay awake all night,

Just trying to cry.

You had to have meant something.

You had to have made your way into my heart.

If you were always there,

Then why am I not falling apart?

Noose

2009

I loved you once, I paid the price.
The same mistake, my demise.

I can't help running back, just to hear your voice.
Poison to my heart, my choice.

Self-destruction make me whole.
Your dangerous kiss fuels my soul.

The pain you bring stings like hell.
But look at me, can you tell?

I beg for your punishment, for your abuse.
You're the only one.
My noose.

No More Love Songs
2009

I don't want to write a love song.

But if I wrote a love song,

It would be so long.

And it'd be about you.

I don't want to write a love song.

No kissy-kiss, "I love you."

But if I wrote a love song,

It would be so long,

And it'd be about you.

Baby, you got me like no other.

Love you more 'cause you're a mother.

I'd love to tell you this in every-way.

So, I'll just tell you every-day.

But I don't want to write a love song,

'cause if I wrote a love song, it would be so long;

It'd be about you.

Consume Me

2009

I want to look at you like Johnny looked at June.

I want to walk the line, just say that you'll be mine.

I want to feel that yearning, feel the ring burning.

Let your fire consume me.

Consume me.

I won't take my guns to town.

No Sunday morning coming down.

I won't wear only black, if you take me down to Jack.

I won't say that it ain't me babe, a ghost rider I won't be.

If you let your fire consume me.

Consume me.

You've confused me, now consume me, take me or let me
go but let me know!

If you'll let me look at you, like Johnny looked at June. Let
me look at you, let me be consumed.

Heroes

2010 – 22 years old

(but you knew that, you've been paying attention, right?!?)

I have a lot of heroes in my life. I can't possibly have just one.

Just hear me out a minute and then I will be done.

My heroes aren't firefighters or cops,

Although I appreciate all they do.

My heroes are people I know and love and one of them is you.

I respect you and admire you.

Because I know that you are strong.

I trust you and look up to you, because you've been there all along.

If ever our lives may truly part,

Know that you're always in my heart.

When you're lost and know nothing, know this...

My Friend, My Hero...somewhere you are missed.

Once Upon a Time
2010

Once upon a time I lived a life.

Once upon a time I lived a lie.

She gave me shelter and showed me a way.

Although lacking, I suppose it was okay.

Once upon a time, I floated in every way.

Once upon a time I drifted in every way.

She let me go and so I stayed.

Although unhappy I suppose I was sane.

Once upon a time I settled for less.

Once upon a time I settled for second best.

She wasn't "the one" and now that it's through,

Although it is tough I suppose I will start anew.

Once upon a time I decided I don't need that.

Once upon a time, I chose, and I won't go back.

Smile

2010

A smile is simple, a smile is true.

A smile is honesty, that's what I want from you.

Smile for me, smile for you.

Smile for truth, that's what I want from you.

A smile is pure, a smile is not reviewed.

A smile is trusted, that's what I want from you.

Smile just to smile, smile so strong.

Smile for love, smile when it's gone.

A smile is beauty, a smile is not abused.

A smile is happiness, that's what I want for you.

Smile when your heart breaks.

Smile when it's whole.

Smile when you think of me.

Smile when you don't.

These Wings

2010 (For Jake)

For eternity I will be by your side.

When you see blackness in the sky, don't fear it.

Know it is my wings spread wide, shielding you forever
from this cruel world's lies.

I shall spread these blackened wings like a dark angel from
the abyss.

If you are certain of nothing else, know this:

These wings will protect you;

My love: comfort you;

My truths: guide you.

Your pain shall never be yours alone.

I will deny my place at Heaven's gate to take on, myself,
your eternal fate.

Evil may scab these wings, but never your heart.

Wherever you are, I will never be too far.

I may carry the world on my back, but I will always hold
you highest.

Forever you have nothing to fear.

Always, I am here.

A Warm Blanket (enough said)
2010

A warm blanket, that's all you want.
No warm in your heart or warm in your head.
You just want warm in your bed.
Enough said.

A guide, a shelter, a protection.
No care or truth or discretion.
A warm blanket, that's all you want.
It's spirituality that you dread.
On uneven ground, never will you tread.
Enough said.

I am but a mortal, with flaws.
Trapped for too long in your jaws.
A warm blanket, that's all you want.
No emotion to be read.
Only a heart as heavy as lead.
Enough said.

No warm in your mind, spirit, or soul.

Sights set only on material goals.
A warm blanket, that's all you want.
Seeing as my soul was never fed,
This relationship is dead.
Enough said.

Red Dress

2010

In life, or at least in mine, you'll find...

Same places, same faces, same time.

So, when you see the Red Dress, slip in the side door...

Your jaw can't help but to hit the floor.

Now, you have to choose.

It's not yet decided if you'll win or lose.

Follow your desires or to your room retire?

My friend, you should know this...

You can't possibly be quenched without tasting the dish.

Though she'll share a smile, maybe even stay with you a while;

You'll feel fine, but you will find, it's soon right back to real life.

It always comes back to how you react.

Will you survive the test, of the Red Dress, or will she follow you always?

Will you walk the rest of your days in a haze or will you stand to say,

I've seen the Red Dress and I turned away."

I Wish

2010

I wish that you would know, the way that my love grows.

The way your beauty shows, you need to know.

I wish you could see, the way you can be.

The way you amaze me, you need to see.

I wish you could understand, the way you help me stand.

The way you are so grand, you need to understand.

I wish that you would feel, the way my heart, you steal.

The ways you help me heal, you need to feel...

My love.

Pain must make good poetry, 'cause I sure write a lot

2010

My heart, it hurts so much. I wish you would just break it.

You know you already have it. Please just go on and take it.

I don't need it if you're not here. I won't use it if you're not near.

I beg of you, save me from the pain.

Just leave me alone and empty, it's all the same.

You've stopped it time and time again from beating,

I ask you now, please, stop my heart from bleeding.

Photo Credit: Clayton Gomez

Second Guess

2011 - 23 years old

(This year gets loco! You know who you are.)

I'm so tired of being here.

I'm tired of this place.

For every time I close my eyes, I swear I see your face.

This isn't good.

This isn't right.

Neither of us needs this love in our lives.

What is love really?

Is it the words that we say?

Is it what we feel? Is it thinking of you every day?

How can I sleep feeling like this?

All I want is one more kiss.

But that one more kiss, it's just never enough.

Have to take it easy though, I'm not sprung. I'm tough.

"I'll never fall in love again; the relationship thing just isn't for me."

But when I see your smile, I know I want it to be.

Red Moon

2011

See the moon, like my room:

Red, low glow; let you go?

Early in the morning, sun and moon share the sky.

Now the moon shines like fire, like this reckless soul of mine.

Winds blow without target or care.

My eyes show the same, beware.

Red Moon, one of love and yet of pain.

Forgive me this night, show no disdain.

Half there, half hidden;

Never fully forgiven.

My Red Moon and Me.

Black Kiss

2011

I want that which is not mine.

A devilish soul of the worst kind.

A life which is not my own.

A seed that I have not sown.

I want to rapture the forbidden.

Unlock dark secrets that are hidden.

A desire that I must deny.

A fire that I must let die.

I want that which I cannot hold.

Certainly, annihilation of my fragile soul.

A feeling I did not create.

A comfort that's not mine to take.

I want black skies to fill the air.

Steal it away and keep it there.

A fantasy I must dismiss.

A venomous and deadly kiss.

Just Us
2011

Left, or right?

Right or wrong?

Wrong or just?

Just us.

Play or lose?

Lose or win?

Win or bust?

Just us.

Friend or foe?

Foe or love?

Love or lust?

Just us.

Wish or get?

Get or want?

Want or discuss?

Just us.

Scare or stay?

Stay or go?

Go or trust?

Just us.

Careful or wild?

Wild or solid?

Solid or dust?

Just us.

Regardless, simple, still,
always...

Just us.

Wasted Words

2011

I feel like my words were wasted on those who didn't care.
Now that I've found her, true, those words, they just aren't
there.

Thought of love and life I expressed to those who didn't
read. Now that I have her here, my pen, it just won't bleed.

For too long my emotions were spent on those who didn't
feel. Now that I have her here, these people can't even heal.

I feel like my words were wasted on those who couldn't
see. Now that I have her beauty, I hope she'll set me free.

SN: This would be so much more poetic and awesome if I
were referring to myself: my higher and more spiritual self-
showing herself to me but no. At this point I was still in
the ways of seeking validation from others and seeking
purpose in relationship status. It happens. But for the
record, love yourself first and most! It's legit.

Questions

2011

Questions, questions, questions, why can't we ever just let it be?

We want to know when and how and why.

Why can't we just open our eyes and see?

Questions, questions, questions, why can't we ever just accept?

We know they don't have answers.

Why can't we just be inept?

Questions, questions, questions, why can't we ever just let them disappear?

We hold onto them forever sometimes.

Why can't I let them go? No, not even here.

Wise Man

2011

Tell me something, Wise Man, how can you lose
something you've never held as yours?

Tell me something, Wise Man, how can an open space be
sealed so quickly with boards?

Tell me something, Wise Man, how can one run and not
know from what?

Tell me something, Wise Man, how can, so swiftly, a door
just be shut?

Tell me something, Wise Man, how can the intangible
hurt so much?

Tell me something, Wise Man, how can we ever learn to
truly trust?

The Wise Man looks at me, as if I have been caught,

The Wise Man says behind sad eyes,

"My Child, even I, know not."

First Word, First Line, First Time
2011

<u>That</u> spot in my room will never be the same.
Nor will I when I hear your name.
Whether it's real or just a part of a game,
I don't care – no shame.

<u>The</u> way you make me feel, I can't see it as wrong.
All I want is you now.
I can be weak but will be strong.
I don't care, I'll sing my song.

<u>Truth</u> is my soul's constant motivation.
You've introduced me to so much sophistication.
You leaving now would cause great devastation.
I don't care. No more hesitation.

<u>Is</u> this all just a big mistake?
Am I doing this for heartbreak's sake?
Will I become my own disgrace?
I don't care. It's only you I taste.

<u>Here</u>, in this poem, look and you will find the reasons why
I want you, mine.

This matters more than doubts or time.

It's the first word of every first line,

My first time.

Somewhere You Should Be

2011

I can't stop hearing you in my ear.

I can't stop feeling you near.

Everywhere I look around me, I see that's somewhere you should be.

I won't stop telling you that your beauty is searing.

I won't stop explaining how you're so endearing.

Every time it's magic I see, I know that's somewhere you should be.

I can't stop dreaming of your grace.

I can't stop wishing you'd give me your embrace.

Every day these fantasies, I feed, that's somewhere you should be.

I won't stop putting these poems in a pile.

I won't ever stop trying to make you smile.

Every way I see it, with me is somewhere you should be.

Let Passion Burn

2011

You lit the match. I poured the gasoline.

What really does it matter, what it all means?

See, what we wish may never be. At the end of the day, we are still you and me.

Fires may burn wild across the land, but it sure doesn't mean that we have to hold hands.

The world itself will not cease to spin, even if for second, you let me in.

Every day we'll wake up and it will be another day.

What really does it matter, what we have to say?

Because truly, what we wish may never be. At the end of the day, we are still you and me.

Yes, we sparked a flame, but it may only last a while.

For now, let's just – together – enjoy smiles.

The world itself will not cease to turn, even if for a while, we let passion burn.

Over It

2001

Just fill a void, never hold that position.

My place is merely to give passion she's been missin'.

I have too much love, share with far too many.

Never has anyone else been so damn giving.,

Why would that change?

I thought it would hearing her name,

But, no:

Take a place, play a part.

My place was never to hold her heart.

No longer obsessed.

Not upset.

Just over it.

Photo Credit: Clayton Gomez

Stuck

2011

Sometimes I wonder if I've taken advantage too much. If I use my age as merely a crutch.

I'm stuck.

Did I walk away from blessings too many times? Have I crossed that, "happiest days" line?

It's not right.

Just when I think I've learned how to trust, I notice I know not, the difference of love and lust.

I'm stuck.

Do I truly have someone here with honest eyes? Am I forever condemned for not making up my mind?

It's not right.

I wish I knew what times to listen to my mind, heart, or gut. I need to stop wasting time and depending on luck.

I'm stuck.

When will I allow myself to see what's in plain sight? Will I ever really stop living just for the night?

It's not right.

Passion and Intensity

2011

I know who I could, who I should, what would be easy.

But she's not the one to please me.

She's sweet and nice to see, so why is it that we are not
what I need?

Passion and Intensity.

Stable and calming, love streaming. All these good things I
can see.

But she's not of who I've been dreaming.

What we are, it's not bad to be but I am missing that,

Passion and Intensity.

I know I should be leaving. The smart choice, simple, and
seeming. But this could all just be deceiving.

What we are could be cleansing, but there's not enough,

Passion and Intensity

Feel

2011

There's something in her eyes, like blackness at night. You can feel but cannot see, the way she sees through me.

There's a fire in her soul, like the burning of coals. You can feel but cannot see, the way she burns me.

There's wisdom in her speech, like lights lining the midnight streets. You can feel but cannot see, the deadly words she whispers to me.

Poison

2011

How is it that beauty can hurt so much?

Poison in a touch.

How is it that beauty makes us bleed as such?

Poison in a touch.

Don't have to ingest it, simply see:

Such devastation shouldn't be this easy.

How is it that beauty can rip a heart in two?

Poison, it's true.

How is it that beauty, insanity does brew?

Poison, it's true.

Don't have to ingest it, simply see:

Such devastation shouldn't happen to me.

How is it that because can insert such a hook?

Poison in a look.

How is it that with such beauty your whole world can be
shook?

Poison in a look.

Such sweet, delicious poison.

Her Cry

2011

He watched the sun set over the sea.

He saw the light become her eyes.

He noticed, for the first time, her cry.

The waves moved slow but not silent.

The light reflective and right.

She cried.

He stood there in the water astounded.

He felt the power of the tide.

He noticed, for the first time, her cry.

The night was cold and wet.

The air was calm and still, but it lied.

She cried.

He made a choice then and there.

He decided on a vow to make it right.

He noticed he could, so would, cure her cry.

Wonder Why

2011

Have you ever stopped to wonder why?

Have you ever stopped just to cry?

Have you taken the time to know if you're truly satisfied?

Some people are providers.

We are just survivors.

Have you ever stopped to wonder why?

Have you ever stopped to realize?

Have you taken the time to sit and analyze?

Some people are card dealers.

We are just self-healers.

Have you ever stopped to wonder why?

Have you ever stopped just to sigh?

Have you ever taken the time to ponder your life?

Some people are fighters.

We, friends, are just writers.

Saving Ami

2011

The moon is bright. I can almost see the man. Just like, sometimes, I can see your hand. I can see your hand guiding me, directing me, saving me.

The sky is dark, almost black. But there are a few flashing lights, just like I notice sometimes, you brighten up my life; I know you are seeing me, accepting me, saving me.

The sound is nearly silent, what I hear almost my choice. Just like, if I'm lucky, sometimes I hear your voice. I can hear your voice supporting me, inspiring me, saving me.

Each day, little ways, almost impossible to see.

You save me.

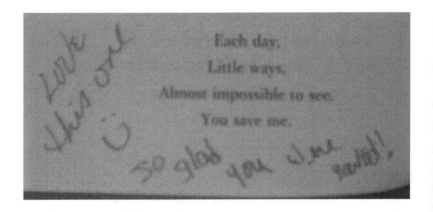

Lying Smile
2011

Your smile lies.
Tapped in time.
No escape from life.

Your tears are true.
Honest, to you.
Fleeing like your youth.

Your eyes still shine.
When they meet mine.
Hoping to be alright.

Your heart is strong.
Beating all along.
It can't be wrong.

The Change

2011

I saw something in your eyes last night that I know I'll
have to crush.

Your feelings suddenly changed.

Now, much more than the common lust.

There was a change in your hands last night, something
different in the way you touched me.

A shift that to me, was screaming.

Danger, I can clearly see.

I felt something in your warmth last night that I know I'll
have to deny.

Your feelings suddenly changed.

Now, we have rules to abide.

There was a change in your heart last night, something
different in the way it beat.

A shift that shook me hard.

Fear that hit me deep.

I heard something in your voice last night, a wish for what cannot be.

Please just turn and run away.

I'll break you.

You won't break me.

You Have Been Warned

2011

Warning! Caution!

Enter my life at high risk.

If you forget all else, don't forget this:

You will fall, and I will run.

This was over far before it was begun,

Warning! Caution!

Is a moment of pleasure worth your pain?

If you don't want to find out, don't call out my name.

You will fall, and I will leave.

A lovely but ever toxic tease.

Warning! Caution!

Danger levels are in the red.

If you don't like to cry, don't lay in my bed.

You will fall, and I will run.

The price you'll pay for being young.

Warning! Caution!

Only broken hearts live here.

If you don't know you're strong enough,
don't even come near.

You will fall, and I will leave.
I'll be fine, as you forget how to breathe.

Work in Progress

2011

I am a work in progress.

This, please, understand. It's not that I don't want to, but I just can't hold your hand.

I am not yet where I want to be.

Time is what I ask from you. It's not that I don't want to but right now I can't be true.

I am constantly changing.

This you can clearly see. It's not that I don't want to, but I don't know yet who to be.

I am a work in progress.

I suppose as are we all. It's not that I don't want to but I'm sorry, I can't catch you if you fall.

Still All About You

2011

Many women, I may want, but what it comes down to is this:

I could have them all, but it'd still be you I miss.

Attention is what I crave, but why? Because it makes me forget that I don't have you at night.

The list goes on and on of the crazy things I do, all just to fill the void of knowing I can't have you.

This way, it's not healthy. I must stop, it's true. Perhaps when I find the right balance, I can be closer to you.

No Good Way to be
2011

Who does my heart belong to?

I sure don't know but it isn't me.

I know not where my love lies.

That's a no-good way to be.

I think I have an idea, but then it could just be a piece.

I know not if I'm even whole and that's a no-good way to
be.

Do I even know what love is?

I guess I'll have to wait and see.

I know not if I've ever seen it.

That's a no-good way to be.

I think I may have glimpsed it and for that, I feel quite
lucky.

I know not what's in my future but that just might be,

An okay way to be.

Wandering Mind

2011

Your face is so poetic.

It makes me feel pathetic.

I can't help it.

When I see you, I see lyrics.

A poem pops instantly in my head.

Of course, my mind always wanders...

To you there in my bed.

Your beauty is such an art.

It's sure to scar my heart.

I can't help it.

When light strikes your eyes, I see paints.

A painting pops instantly in my mind.

Of course, my mind always wanders...

To the next day we'll get to spend time.

You, in your entirety, are so amazing.

Thoughts of you make me crazy.

I can't help it.

When I'm around you, I feel your glow.

A future with you, instantly my fantasy.

Of course, my mind then wanders...

To you always being there next to me.

Super Human

2011

You feel pain, hurt, and doubt?

I thought for so long, these things, you lived without.

I see you as so super human, never with fear in your heart.

I see you as so super human, never seen you fall apart.

You feel disappointment, longing, and trapped?

I thought for so long, you didn't have feelings like that.

I see you as so super human, never with sadness in your
soul.

I see you as so super human, always knowing where you'll
go.

You get lost, tired, and dreary?

I thought for so long, these things you'd never be.

I see you as so super human, never without a path clearly
seen.

I see you as so super human, never perfect but perfect to
me.

You Told Me

2011

You told me to make something, so I made a book.

I ask you now, to give it a look.

Let me know what you think, what you see.

Tell me true, if you enjoy what you read.

You told me that I would be great, in fact, that I already am.

I ask you now to help me make that stand.

Let me know what you think, what you see.

If you still see greatness when you look at me.

You told me I could do anything, I could be whatever I wanted to be.

I ask you now, to share that with me.

Too Special

2011

In your face, I see a glow.
I wish the same was in your soul.
There's brightness in your eyes.
I wish the same was in your life.

You're too beautiful to frown.
You're too amazing to feel down.
You're too special not to know this.

In your smile, I see a need.
I wish the same was in me.
In your walk, I see a graceful sway.
I wish the same was in my way.

You're too beautiful to doubt.
You're too amazing to be without.
You're too special not to know this.

Imagine

2011

All I have to do is see your picture and I write.

Keep staring at it and I'll keep writing all night.

Can you imagine if I had you more in my life?

My hand would cramp. My pen would bleed. You're all I
would need.

I know that I should sleep but I have tried.

I saw you, so now, a poem I must write.

Can you imagine if I had you more in my life?

I'd be writing every emotion. I'd be drained of every
thought. You're all that I could want.

It only takes a second for you to capture my mind.

Even with such distance, it should be a crime.

Can you imagine if I had you more in my life?

I would never stop writing. I would never be able to rest.
Now that, that would be the best.

What It's All About

2011

It's about looking in someone's eyes and seeing them shine.

It's about thinking of that person and smiling every time.

It's about trust beyond compare.

It's about taking on their scary dare.

It's about always wanting to hear their voice.

It's about knowing that there's never really a choice.

It's about beauty you can't describe.

It's about needing them and not knowing why.

It's about never wanting to be without.

It's about never having a single doubt.

It's about this crazy thing called love.

It's about never forgetting the wonders of the above.

WTF DO I KNOW?!

Man did I think I had it all figured out LMFAO

Only You, My Dear

2011

I may share my words with the world. They may even take them on trips.

But only you, My Dear, will hear them from my lips.

Millions may read and understand, but only because you were there to hold my hand.

I may share my words with the world. They may read them to pass the time.

But only you, My Dear, know fully how they're mine.

People may very well enjoy what they read, but only because you were there to push me.

I may share my words with the world, they may realize that they are real.

But only you, My Dear, will ever know how they feel.

Not Mine

2011

Some say words are like daggers but not mine.

Mine are like roses or fine wine.

Some say love is always strong but not mine.

Mine never knows where it lies.

Some say truths are hard to know but not mine.

Mine are quiet but there all the time.

Some say life is a journey but not mine.

Mine is just the blind, leading the blind.

All I Have

2011

All I have is words.

They are far greater then I.

All I have is stories.

They are far more interesting than real life.

I only have these poems as mine.

I want you to have them, cherish them all the time.

All I have is this paper and pen.

They are far greater than I.

All I have is this lead and ink.

They are far more important than my cry.

I only have this book as mine.

I want you to have it, so you'll know I tried.

All I have now is thoughts.

They are far greater than I.

All I have is these feelings.

They are all yours, if you'd like.

Harder Not to Love

2011

Not allowing myself to love is the hardest thing I have ever done.

I turn cold when I have no one to hold.

I lose faith if I don't have a constant kiss to taste.

I want so badly to say, "I love you," hear it back and know it's true.

Always wanting, but not knowing who. Waiting for her is the hardest thing I'll ever do.

Here, then gone, one then none. Living this life is the hardest thing I've ever done.

Loving myself first and only, choosing me over you, is the hardest but most important, thing I'll ever do.

Prayer

2011

All I have are words on paper.

Never out of my mouth.

It gets so frustrating!

I wish I could speak up even now.

I wish someone would steal this pen.

Take it away and lock it up!

Make me use my voice, get me out of this slump.

Get to me to a safe place.

Someone please, bring me salvation.

Show me somewhere I can speak, without any hesitation.

Without making me crazy, take these poems.

They have become me and I, them.

I can't let the written word be all I have.

To be more is my lonesome prayer, Amen.

Get Out and Into

2011

I could write forever about the moon.

Stare at it, embrace it, enjoy it.

But while I write, I still come back to you.

It's low, it's bright, it's white or it's red.

I see these things but you're still in my head.

Get out of my head and into my bed!

I could write forever about the truth.

Think about it, analyze it, enjoy it.

But while I write, I still come back to you.

Its power, I can feel as right.

I see these things, but you're still in my mind.

Get out of my head and into my life!

You, Too

2011

Too dark, too quiet, too still.
For a simple touch, I'd kill.

My heart, my pulse, they beat to the tick of a lonely clock.
I want so badly to hide these thoughts.

Too cold, too lonely, too sad a day.
For your simple smile, I'd run away.

My truther, my emotions, they flow like a wild tide.
I want so badly to deny these feelings of mine.

Too hard, too intense, too much.
Just for your simple love, I'd deny any lust.

My love, my all, they wait for you to come.
I want so badly for this all to be done.

Living in Sin

2011

I think I see something there...

I can't really tell.

It's not clear.

How long has it been?

I think I see that you care...

I can't really be sure.

It's not clear.

How do you think this will end?

Living in Sin.

Sting Me

2011

Why do you have to be so beautiful?

Why do you have to look at me?

It stings. You sting me.

Why do we talk just to talk?

Why does it rarely mean anything?

It stings. You sting me.

Why do you not know what you want?

Why don't you stop to see?

It stings. You sting me.

Why do we pretend it will be okay?

Why doesn't it make sense for us to be?

It stings. You sting me.

Why are you so damn perfect?

Why can't I be what you need?

It stings. You sting me.

Never Ending Story
2011

You love me now, but is it because you are alone?

What's going to happen when the other comes home?

Will your love still be with me?

Will changes be made so 'we' can be?

How long until we again share a kiss?

I just don't see an end to this.

I love you always, not just when I'm lonely.

One day I only dream, that you will hold me only.

Hopefully your love will never truly stray.

In time, we'll find our escape, our way.

Soon we will dance in the dark again,

Never will it really be our end.

Changing

2011

Thoughts turn into dreams.

That's true.

All I have are dreams now, not you.

Not that I ever did.

Who am I trying to kid?

Whether it's real or pretend, I'm thankful in the end.

Dreams turn into aspirations.

That's true.

All I have are goals now, not you.

That's more than I had before.

It seems you've opened a hidden door.

Whether this is it or there's more,

It's now and you I'm thankful for.

Goals turn into success.

It's true.

All I have is a better me, thanks to you.

I am Them

2011

A line in the sky looks like a pen.

It cuts right through.

Might as well be my skin.

While most bleed blood, I bleed words and ink.

They are all I have. I am them, they are me.

Wrinkles in a paper look like a vein.

They are forever flowing.

Might as well mark me insane.

While most feel: words and poems, I see.

They are all I have. I am them. They are me.

My pulse is instead a poetic line, consuming my heart.

Forever beating strong and long.

Might as well tear me apart.

While most love....

This writing is my only way of being.

They are all I have.

I am them, they are me.

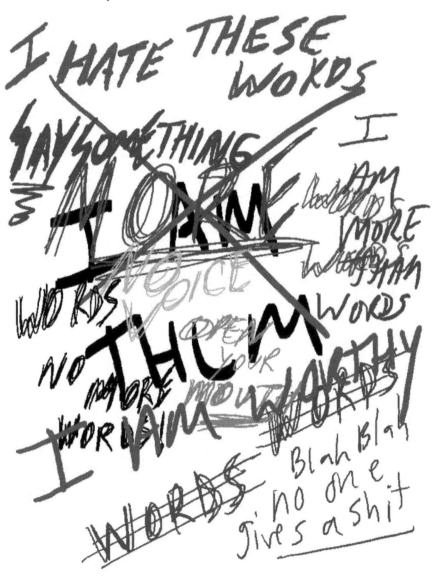

Insanity

2011

Ever wonder how track runners can run the same circle over and over again?

I did...but then there was you.

Insanity is doing the same, expecting a different result.

That's where I am beat. It's that consistency, I seek.

The sooner I accept things will never change, the better off I'll be.

When I can accept that you are no good for me.

That is all easier said than done, my Friend.

I want so bad for it to be you and me...

51-50.

Insanity.

Frozen Soul

2011

I hate the cold.

It reminds me of a dark time in my life.

A time...when I'm sure I deserved to die.

I sigh.

It makes me yearn to love and be loved.

And right now, I have neither of the above.

I hate the snow.

It reminds me of that dark night.

A night when I was sure, I deserved to die.

I sigh.

It makes me yearn for closeness, a hero.

And right now, I have no one, zero.

I hate the winter winds.

It reminds me of the blackened place.

A place where I was sure, I deserved to die.

I sigh.

Belong

2011

Smiles lie.

As do eyes and words.

It's up to us if we learn, to realize that we live in different worlds.

There was a time war was waged over a woman.

A man would lose all he had just for love's chance.

Maybe I belong more, in a place like that.

Touches lie.

As do kisses and hugs.

It's up to us if we learn, to realize it's best to run.

There was a time romance ruled supreme.

All that mattered was love at last.

Maybe I belong more, in time like that.

People lie.

As do actions and non.

It's up to us if we learn, to realize where we truly belong.

Today, I Know

2011

Today, I know...

I love you Lady, too much it seems.
I wonder if those around me can see,
If they can see through me.
Today, I know, you do.
You see into my soul, it's true.

Today, I know...
I miss you, Woman, too strongly I think.
I wonder if those around me can see,
If they, too, know what you do to me.
Today, I know, you do.
You see my pain, it's true.
Today, I know...
I dream of you, Beautiful, too often I dream.
I wonder if those around me can see.
If they experience this journey with me.

Today, I know, you do.
You feel it too, true?

Nothing More

2011

I want nothing more than my hand to caress your cheek.

For those captivating eyes, to look at me.

I want nothing more than my touch to explore.

For those gentle lips that are only yours.

I want nothing more than to gently move your hair from your face.

For those healing haven to take me to a better place.

I want nothing more than my lips to make you smile.

For those loving arms to wrap me up for a while.

I want nothing more than to be tangled in your skin.

For those amazing gifts, I'd never want another again.

IDK

2011

I don't know if I'm more afraid of your "no" or of your "yes".

Too bad for me, there's no easy test.

I don't know if I'm more afraid or your "goodbye" or your kiss.

So sad for me, there's no easy way to know this.

I don't know if I'm more afraid of your silence or your words.

Too tough for me, there's no easy way to learn.

I don't know if I'm more afraid of your love or your 'not to be'.

Lucky for me, there is one way to see.

It's not easy, but easy has never been good to me.

Dinner for Two

2011

I lit the match, but you poured the gas.

You're just as responsible as I.

This never would've happened if you didn't come to me that night.

If your lips never met mine, but alas... tonight we dine.

With candles lit in a place which few get,

See the small flame, smell its scent.

This night, like the other, we'll not soon forget.

Souls that meet this way, can't lie.

They instead, dance darkly, like tonight...we dine.

Red wine, like our lust, flows freely.

Entering our bodies and taking control.

I know that it's already taking its toll.

This night, like the other, we may hide away like a troll....

Can't say we didn't try...

Merely that for tonight, we dine.

Gazes traded back and forth from me to you, you to me.

Thoughts that will never, could never, be unleashed.,

See though to what will not ever be.

This night, like the other, peels my heart like a rind.

But tonight, we dine.

Tomorrow matters not, now as soft music feels our heads.

Fear not the repercussions of our bed.

On this night, like the other, I'll wait there dead.

Before you say its time, to say goodbye....

So tonight, please, let us dine.

F This World

2011

Fear is the ultimate weakness.

Unsure of truths, we go.

Children are taught to face it.

Keep strong, they say, just to find our names in stone.

The end we cannot, nor should try to escape.

Healing even, it could be.

In eternity may we only rest.

So, all of life, we won't miss thee.

Words or script may guide us.

Or perhaps, even lead us astray.

Really the end is not to be feared.

Life is our biggest dismay.

Dying will be our only freedom, let us welcome that day.

(there's that ideation again)

Truth

2011

I don't know why I ask you for the truth.
You give it to me, every time.
I suppose I am hoping you'll change your mind.
That, in time, you'll see you could be mine.

My hands hurt.
My eyes burn.
I wish I would learn.
The truth hurts.

I don't know why I ask you for your thoughts.
You've shared them with me all along.
I suppose I'm just hoping certain thoughts are gone.
That, in time, you'll see that I could love you forever on.

My chest burns.
My heart cries.
I wish I could realize,
The truth is blind.

I don't know why I ask you for your all.

You've already sworn it to another.,

I suppose I am hoping, you'll choose me – your lover.

That, in time, you'll see...I am like no other.

My soul lingers, my love inept.

I wish I could just accept...The truth is all that's left.

Your Words

2011

"If she's worth it, you'll wait," you say.

But how long must I sacrifice?

When does loneliness count for more?

Will it ever be enough to suffice?

"Be patient and don't run away," you request.

But how long must I play this waiting game?

When will she see what I mean?

Will she ever admit she feels the same?

"If you can't handle it, then stop," you suggest.

But how long can I fight this feeling?

When will I move on?

Will I ever be able to replace her with healing?

"If she's worth it, wait, if not, then don't," you restate.

But how long must I go back and forth?

When will I finally decide?

Will this love ever just take its course?

Dear Friends,

The part of writing that you don't see: after writing a lot last night I was overcome with emotion and had a complete breakdown. I cried a violent cry for a long time. I prayed to Mom long and hard through sobs. I fell asleep on the couch in my office because I was too weak after to walk to my bed. I know that I needed that, but it is not easy. Re-writing this book has been the greatest, most intense, therapeutic, and heart-breaking experience. I was in such a hurry last time, to beat my Mom's cancer and publish before it took her, that I did not really sit with it much. Even after it was published, I did not read it until now. I suppose in that way I have always been one to "work through" things by writing a poem and "moving on." Because I never faced these things before, I have carried them with me. Even though I have tried releasing in other ways, I haven't been able to. I realized this morning that being present in this re-write, reading and re-reading and allowing myself to be vulnerable to my own words...that is my mission, my lesson right now. Acknowledging, really, my experiences and the pain is important. I usually down play my past, but I have been angry; I have been hurt so deeply; I have been through some really fucked up shit and I have a right to feel all of that. You do too. I have the right to own my own story and as I share it more, now with you I feel that energy surging through me. This is the path to true healing for me, thank you for being with me for this. I hope it can help you heal too or perhaps inspire your own journey to owning your story, and giving power, permission, to your feelings.

Fading Images

2011

I imagine waking in a different way:

On a brighter day,

In a foreign place,

Next to your smiling face.

I imagine loving you but at what cost?

My images fade and now I am lost.

I imagine coming back to a different home:

A spot I know,

Never really alone,

Hearing your sweet voice on my phone.

I imagine loving you but at what cost?

My images fade and now I am lost.

I imagine sleeping in a different bed:

My soul fed,

Not a moment of dread,

Feeling yours next to my head.

I imagine loving you but at what cost?

My images fade and now I'm just lost.

Come See Me

2011

Come see me, at our imaginary house in the clouds. Where we can be together, without any doubts.

Come see me, in our fictional room high in the sky. Where we can be together without having to hide.

Comes see me in our fabricated bed of air. Where we can be together with no worry or cares.

Come see me anytime day or night. Until then, the seconds I'll count,

At our imaginary house in the clouds.

Love is Love is Love is You

2011

It's 37 degrees.

I'm wondering what you think of me.

Questioning if possible, but not easy, will really come to be.

If you can truly see...

Love isn't chosen and cannot lie.

Love decides who you fall for but not why.

Love is more powerful than you or I.

Love is the one thing more lasting than life.

It's icy enough to snow.

I'm wondering if you'll let go.

Questioning if "us" is happening too fast or too slow.

Will we continue to talk of places we'll go?

If you and I will come to know...

Love is our light in the dark.

Love keeps us from falling apart.

Love that is worth it, is hard.

Love is why with you, I have no guard.

It's dark, lonely, and cold.

I'm wondering if you and I will grow old.

Questioning if we're strong enough to be so bold.

Will our fragile hearts crumble and fold?

If you'll ever truly hear what you're being told...

Love is what I feel for you.

Love is to what I will be true.

Love is all I know to do.

Love is love is love...

Is you.

(or so I'm told 😉)

If I Do

2011

I have no right to love you.

You've given me no reason, no rhyme.

Only a little time.

I've never wanted someone so much, so this time if I do,

I'm glad it's you.

I have no right to kiss you.

You didn't give me permission to get that close.

Only, almost.

I've never felt like I couldn't just walk away, so this time if
I do, I'm glad it's you.

I have no right to hold you.

You didn't give me more than lust.

Only, maybe once.

I've never felt lasting pain, so this time if I do,

I'm glad it's you.

I have no right to care about you.

You've given me no commitment, no heart.

Only, perhaps a part.

I've never wanted to try so much, so this time if I do,

I'm glad it's you.

I have no right to love you.

You've given me no signal, no sign.

But I love you anyway, all the time.

I've never had my heart broken, so this time if I do,

I'm glad it's you.

I'm just so glad it's you.

(Now doesn't that last part seem a bit contradictory to, I don't know, this whole fucking book?! Never been heart-broken? Yeah, ooook. Lies. That's me trying to be tough and stuff, like I do. But whatevs.)

More Than a Night

2011

Maybe one day, when it's time – when it's right,

You'll let me love you for more than a night.

If not, I guess that's okay. I still go on loving you, until my dying day.

Maybe one day, when it's time – when it's right,

You'll let me hold you for more than a night.

If not, I guess that's alright. I'll still miss you, every night.

Maybe one day when it's time – when it's right,

You'll let me be yours for more than a night.

If not, I guess that's fine. I'll still know that for you, I tried.

Miss Teresa

2012

On this day, even Heaven shed a tear.

What's left now is to live for her, with no fear.

We shared together good times and bad.

What's left now are the memories we have.

Live your life for what's right.

What's left now is to smile for her, all the time.

Know that there's strength such as hers.

What's left now is to remember with our hearts and words.

Today we say we love you so, Miss Teresa,

What's left now is not goodbye,

But we'll see ya.

But

2012

I love you...

But you'll be gone again tomorrow.

A moment of bliss for a lifetime of sorrow.

Some say no one knows but you do.

You know how I feel, you feel it too.

I love you...

But every night I sleep alone.

With you I am happy, even though I should,

I'm not strong enough to let you go.

Soul Searching

2012

I want to take you to a dark place.

Where you can't see a thing but an Angel's face.

At the Universe's core, second life is born.

You can't see her, but you can feel her smile.

All the while,

Dark, damp, and hot.

Souls swimming in a melting pot.

Where's yours? Can it be found?

.....

Look down.

Love, "Snuggie"

2012

Slow down. Look around. Remember to breathe it in.

It's a journey, Love, not the end.

Try your best to smile, sing, dance, and laugh.

Cherish the little moments, make them last.

I made it my mission to remind you of these,

Now for the list of what you've given to me:

You very quickly proved that I do still have a heart.

Taught me I can't be afraid to step into the dark.

I can't describe the ways you bring me peace.

Such pure happiness, to say the least.

What's better than loving is being loved.

I know this now because of the below and above.

You'll never know how great it is to simply just be.

To look into your eyes and feel loved for being me.

You've shown me to be happy and that's more than okay.

With you I find more about me, every single day.

I was not expecting to find someone as wonderful as you.

Now that I have, here's what I plan to do:

Every second we're together, I'll make the world disappear.

Take every change I can to have you near.

Making you happy, making memories of us,

The only importance is your love, your trust.

One verse is not near enough to tell you what I'll do.

This poem isn't enough for all the ways I'll love you.

Panda Bear

2012

How others see you, I don't really care.

As long as you'll be, My Panda Bear.

Where we are in life, I really don't care.

As long as I have, My Panda Bear.

What goes on in the world, I really don't care.

As long as standing next to me, is My Panda Bear.

When storms may come, I really don't care.

As long as you stay, My Panda Bear.

Why all of this happened, I really don't care.

As long as you're always, My Panda Bear.

Funny story about that: I don't know if you caught on by now or not but! SPOILER ALERT! I'm a lesbian. Didn't see that coming, right? I know, crazy.

Anyway, I have never dated a lesbian. I know, what?!? So, look, shit happens. Straight women meet an awesome little lesbian like myself and decide to give it a try, fall in love, so on and so forth.

Google homoromantic if you're really interested.

Remember that #singlelife from before? Still accurate SOOO you see how well this has worked out for me, just saying. Not the point.

The point is, my girlfriend at this time was straight and we had a conversation about how I do not care about that. That being with me does not require her to start identifying a different way or as gay/bi/whatever.

My words were: I don't care if you identify as a God damned panda bear, so long as you're good to me and love me. And thus, the nickname and subsequent sexual identity of hers was born. It still makes me laugh that after that she took on panda bear as her sexual orientation, no one got it.

Fun times.

Moral of the story: your orientation is yours alone, fuck the rest; live your truth!

Reminder

2012

Before all else, remember this:
Anything that can be broken can be fixed.

You can schedule and all, you can make all of your lists.
You are but a human, one person, with a wish.

When it's going all wrong, remember this:
Anything that can be broken, can be fixed.

You can feel so out of control, you can run crazy all day.
You can lose your mind a bit, just know it'll be okay.

At times you may feel hopeless, but remember this:
Anything that can be broken, can be fixed.

You can give your all and more, you can get someone's
back in return.
You can be disappointed, either way, you learn.

Where life exists, remember this:

Anything that can be broken, can be fixed.

Don't forget to breathe.

Don't forget to laugh.

Don't forget that it's your happiness, that helps make others last.

Fun Fact: I coached high school girls' basketball for a couple of years back from 2010-2012 and it was one of the highlights of my life.

We didn't win much, but boy did I have some talented young women! I am happy to report that many went off to college, one is a Sheriff now and I got to be her reference – so cool for me! I ran into one of the most talented players I have ever known at the gym the other day. She's local and working hard and makes me so proud.

I saw a ton of myself in those girls. I know they will be alright, they are resilient too. I am incredibly proud of each and every one of my players. They gave their hearts and souls out there every night. They are warriors in everything they do, then and now.

I also got to work with and council young people in schools, queer and non-queer. Those students taught me so much more than I could ever explain.

Watch, "The Bad Kids" on Netflix.

They all helped inspire the next poem.

To all of my kids, you know who you are, and this next poem is yours.

Love, Miss Ami/Coach Davis.

The Other Side of Agony

2014

They say, "it gets better," but in the dark, we cannot see:

The other side of agony.

They say, "hold on, my child," but they don't see how we
are disgusted by their apathy, with no hope of

The other side of agony.

They say, "you'll make it through this," but they don't
know how hard it is just to be. It feels like there is no,

Other side of agony.

They say, "I don't understand. There were no signs," but
we silently scream tragedy! I know we can't see it always,

The other side of agony.

They say...it doesn't matter what *they* say.

We are full of beautiful majesty.

I promise you, there is "the other side" of agony.

We are, the other side of agony.

The other Side of Agony expansion (3/9/18)

I hear oh by Ami what about what *they* say?

Who cares what *they* say? I say,

Who are they anyway??

They are merely extras in the movie of your life. You can do with them or without them, that's your right. To write...

Your story is yours alone.

Darkness can only come if you agree to dim your light.

What about what they say? Who are they anyway?

You. You and I. We are the truth. Life and love are the truth.

So how can we be told that what we do in love is wrong when that is the only absolute?

My friends, please take care to pick the right tree when seeking to digest its fruit.

Let us not continue to believe in what they say, let us not continue to be what they say but instead embrace fully our true selves because we are the truth.

We are love.

We are the other side...of agony.

Don't you dare tell me that you are not enough.

Do not tell me that because of your life you cannot succeed or because of your past you cannot go on.

Don't you dare tell me that you can't possibly be...

The other side of agony.

Do not even for half a second pretend to believe that you will not be great.

Everything you do, every step, every breath that you take –

Make it hard to hate.

Live in love

Share yourself with the world in a way they cannot take,

You are already great.

If anyone says otherwise, just know that is blasphemy!

You are, we are, the other side of agony.

These creative juices are flowing through me now, let them try to tell me to be quiet or sit down –

Whatever they thought they took from me, I have found.

It is here, and it is now, and it is me and it is you, it is our voice; that beautiful sound.

We are the truth.

We are love.

Listen. Please.

NO matter what they do, no matter what say or try to tell you; whatever lie they try to sell or try to make you believe just promise me something:

Promise me that you will reject it, that you will rebel.

That you will not fall into their trap, that you will rise above that and be you because you are the truth. You are love. The truth is you and the truth is me.

The truth in our stories.

Do not be confused, though, our stories are not all of us. We are made of so much more. We are made of love and of light –

And if we do things right –

We will find our tribe.

When you find that tribe you must rise.

Rise together and lift each other, UP.

SO that whatever they say –

We can interrupt.

We are not our experiences solely, we are not our past. No matter what we've been through WE are not tragedy. We are love.

Love.

That is you.

And that is me.

And that...

Is the other side of agony.

Photo Credit: Clayton Gomez

With Love, From Ami:

I wanted to end it here. I wanted The Other Side of Agony to be where I left you, because it is beautiful and true.

Now, I don't think that would be fair and considering Mom is a big part of this, so too, should be her poem.

Angel

2014

She wears white.

A long, beautiful gown.

Victorian.

Her locks are long.

Lightly curled and trimmed.

Red.

She has a softness.

A gentle face.

Kind.

Her presence is cold.

Her heart warm.

Guiding.

She is my mother's angel.

A guardian to her.

Light.

"I am not what happened to me, I am what I choose to become." – Carl Gustav Jung

Repeat after me:

I choose to be authentic.

I choose to be strong.

I choose to be heard.

I choose to accept that I am powerful and peaceful.

I choose to accept my purpose in the world.

I choose to not accept failure, defeat, or negativity.

I choose to not allow my voice to be muzzled.

I choose to do what's right.

I choose to do what my heart wants done.

I choose to love myself unconditionally.

I choose to love others unconditionally.

I choose to share that love and light with the world.

Because I am kind.

Because I am smart.

Because I belong of the world.

How about you? Now it's your turn!

Fill these out! If you need to "phone a friend" for help, go ahead.

I choose to be...

_____

_____

I choose to accept or allow...

_____

_____

I choose to not accept or allow...

_____

_____

I choose to do...

_____

_____

I love me because....

(to get you started)...Awesome!

Courageous, Strong, Amazing, Talented, Spirited

_____

_____

_____

I love you all, Dearly. You are my heroes. My inspiration. Thank you for you! #SOMUCHLOVE

Forever Yours, -Ami, Of The People.

"Don't determine your life by comparing yourself with others. It is because we are different that each of us is special. Don't set your goals by what others deem important. Only you know what is best for you. Don't take for granted the things closest to your heart; cling to them as you would your life, for without them life is meaningless. Don't let your life slip through your fingers by living in the past or for the future. By living your life one day at a time you will live all the days of your life. Don't give up when you still have something to give. Nothing is really over until the moment you stop trying. Don't be afraid to encounter risks. It's by taking chances that we learn to be brave. Don't shut love out of your life by saying it's impossible to find. The quickest way to find love is to give love. The fastest way to lose love is to hold it too tightly and the best way to keep love is to give it wings. Don't dismiss your dreams. To be without dreams is to be without purpose. Don't run through life so fast that you forget not only where you've been but also where you were going. Life isn't a race, but a journey to be savored each step of the way."

-Author Unknown

To all of the people I have been blessed to work with; to all of the young people/students especially. You are my kids. Once you're mine, you're always mine.
Thank you for helping me grow and learn.
THANK YOU for existing, so that I might find my true purpose, my true calling.
I am forever indebted to each and every one of you.
I love you.
My next book is just for you.
See you in, "Make it Hard to Hate." -2019

-Miss Ami

ESSPECIAL SHOUT OUTs AND THANK YOUs:

To my siblings: life has a funny way of fucking things up, I know. But you were always there for me and you were right there through this, although this is my perspective I want to acknowledge, and I want readers to know, that I have 2 older sisters and a baby brother who have their own sides to this very same story.

Tina, thank you for being the protector and provider even though you were so young and shouldn't have had to.

Krystal, thank you for being the caregiver and rock that none of us could've been when Mom needed it most.

Alex (Brother, because it's just weird to actually use your real name), words will never describe accurately how much I love you and how proud I am. You are and always have been a hero of mine. As fucked up as our family is, I love you all so much and I am so grateful for you.

Dad, (Rick Andrews) I know we have been through a lot, but I couldn't be more proud or happy to be your daughter. You define strength and authenticity. You are always 110% yourself and that inspires me so much. I can't wait to see how we continue to grow closer and the adventures we will get into together! You are my favorite adrenaline junkie and sender of care packages. I love you.

Sonia Sanchez for putting up with my shenanigans for all of these years! You have been my best friend, my confidant, my teacher (in so many ways), and my consistent, "fuck her, her loss – here's a beer" buddy for damn near my whole life. No one else could do it, I'm sure. I am eternally grateful for you and your family. F is for Friends who do stuff together!

Rich Sparks for believing in me all along. Without you I could never have ended up where I am. Thank you for not giving up on me! For all the "come to Jesus meetings," the redirections, the guidance, the lessons, and support. You gave me so many more chances that I deserved and that has shaped my life so much. You are and will forever be my pseudo-dad as I am honored to be your "son" (hehe) – inside joke, people.

Melissa Woods for being my rock so many times. For always giving me a safe place to be belligerently drunk, bitch about whatever I need to, to get lost in music, to laugh my ass off and to cry honestly but not alone. Your support and love mean the world to me, being with you is such a happy place for me!

Julie and Mike Fontana who opened me up to becoming spiritually and physically strong. Although our paths change, the lessons learned have not. I am eternally grateful for your catalyst in my life. You helped spark a flame. Thank you.

(Editors, contributors, and overall definition of badassness):

Tess Ponce for inspiration, editing, quotes, and never saying in so many words that I'm wrong. I appreciate you letting me figure that one out for myself ☺ Always more than a friend, never less than family. To the entire Ponce family for teaching me, guiding me, supporting me; for being my family of choice, my home. You'll never know what you all truly mean to me. For the record, Tess is the O.G. 25 Years editor, HOLLA!

Erin Hill for connecting, editing, and providing multiple perspectives; for sharing your journey with me, encouraging me to explore mine, and listening to all my, "dude, crazy shit just happened" stories. My human, spiritual journey journal. Love.

Natasha Hillenburg for always being the smile, laugh, sarcastic comment that I need; for editing and encouraging me with this re-write and for being my future podcast co-host because, well, we are fucking funny together! Most thoughtful person on the planet!

Anne-Michelle Meyer for putting up with my awkwardness and making beautiful art from it. Thank you so much for you, your friendship, your model of strength, and the photos in this book. Look her up for some legit photo sessions, people!

Clayton Gomez for your awesome pics and letting me use them! Thank you for your contribution and support!

My guides, my supports, my friends, my lovers: Blake & Alexis, Marie, Jon & Fam, Katie, Family & Gals, Hillary & Liz, Kim, "other" Kim, Tabitha, Tiffany, Nicole, Dan, Trisha, Mattie, Anamarie, my beautiful niece Taylor, Rachel, "Dollface", "Kiid", all of the nurses and doctors that helped my Mom and helped us through it, so many more!

If I were to list every single amazing, life-changing, supportive person in my life, this book would be 100 pages of that. I am so blessed that way! Please know that I love you and appreciate you all, even if I have not written it here. Hopefully, you know.

I am so blessed to have so many people through the years who have loved me, supported me, guided me, and just been so amazing. I can't tell you how much I love and appreciate each and every one of you. Thank you for you! #SOMUCHLOVE

About the Author

Ami Davis has been writing since she was about eight years old. Well, you know, more than just her barely legible name. She began to keep close to those writings at age fourteen when she realized what an outlet it was. (Side-note: it is super awkward to write about yourself in third person. Anyway, ONWARD!)

Ami uses writing as a positive coping mechanism and hopes to encourage others to do so as well.

Ami's goal with this publication is to reach out to people, especially the young; the queer; the hurting; the lost; and those that feel they are not heard to let them know they are not alone and that their past, their raising, their environment does not define them. As she did, they can rise-up from hardship and trauma to become successful in their own right. Ami hopes to encourage more young people to put forth to the world their views, their feelings, their experiences and to guide all folks to intersecting with one another in a loving, compassionate, healing way.

Her message: "I never want someone to feel sorry for me or what I've been through, but I do hope readers will remember these words, and perhaps, walk with a little more care through their lives; share a smile, save a life."

Connect with me!

Instagram: @theamidavis

Facebook: Ami Davis

Snapchat: Amizzle1445

Made in the USA
Columbia, SC
14 May 2019